FIX IT QUICK

ONE DISH

Publications International, Ltd.

Favorite Brand Name Recipes at www.fbnr.com

Pictured on the front cover *(clockwise from top left):* Delicious Ham and Cheese Puff Pie *(page 86),* Apple Curry Chicken *(page 48),* Saffron Chicken & Vegetables *(page 42)* and Vegetable Casserole *(page 92).*

Pictured on the back cover: Smoked Salmon Hash Browns *(page 8).*

ISBN-13: 978-1-4127-2731-0
ISBN-10: 1-4127-2731-6

Library of Congress Control Number: 2007935575

Manufactured in China.

8 7 6 5 4 3 2 1

Microwave Cooking: Microwave ovens vary in wattage. Use the cooking times as guidelines and check for doneness before adding more time.

Preparation/Cooking Times: Preparation times are based on the approximate amount of time required to assemble the recipe before cooking, baking, chilling or serving. These times include preparation steps such as measuring, chopping and mixing. The fact that some preparations and cooking can be done simultaneously is taken into account. Preparation of optional ingredients and serving suggestions is not included.

table of contents

italian sausage and vegetable stew

1 pound hot or mild Italian sausage links, cut into 1-inch pieces
1 package (16 ounces) frozen vegetable blend, such as onions and green, red and yellow bell peppers
2 medium zucchini, sliced
1 can (about 14 ounces) diced Italian-style tomatoes
1 jar (4½ ounces) sliced mushrooms, drained
4 cloves garlic, minced

1. Brown sausage in large saucepan over medium-high heat 5 minutes; drain fat.

2. Add frozen vegetables, zucchini, tomatoes, mushrooms and garlic; bring to a boil. Reduce heat; cover and simmer 10 minutes. Cook, uncovered, 5 to 10 minutes or until slightly thickened. *Makes 6 servings*

Serving Suggestion: Serve with garlic bread.

Prep and Cook Time: 30 minutes

italian sausage and vegetable stew

mac and cheese toss

8 ounces oven baked deli ham, diced
4 cups (1 quart) prepared deli macaroni and cheese
½ cup frozen green peas, thawed
¼ cup milk or cream

1. Combine all ingredients in microwavable 2-quart casserole. Toss gently yet thoroughly to blend. Cover with plastic wrap.

2. Microwave on HIGH 3 minutes; stir. Microwave 1 minute more or until heated through. *Makes 4 servings*

Note: To thaw peas quickly, place peas in a small colander and run under cold water 15 to 20 seconds or until thawed. Drain well.

oriental chicken & rice

1 (6.9-ounce) package RICE-A-RONI® Chicken Flavor
2 tablespoons margarine or butter
1 pound boneless, skinless chicken breasts, cut into thin strips
¼ cup teriyaki sauce
½ teaspoon ground ginger
1 (16-ounce) package frozen Oriental-style mixed vegetables

1. In large skillet over medium heat, sauté rice-vermicelli mix with margarine until vermicelli is golden brown.

2. Slowly stir in 2 cups water, chicken, teriyaki sauce, ginger and Special Seasonings; bring to a boil. Reduce heat to low. Cover; simmer 10 minutes.

3. Stir in vegetables. Cover; simmer 5 to 10 minutes or until rice is tender and chicken is no longer pink inside. Let stand 3 minutes. *Makes 4 servings*

Variation: Use pork instead of chicken and substitute ¼ cup orange juice for ¼ cup of the water.

Prep Time: 5 minutes
Cook Time: 25 minutes

mac and cheese toss

smoked salmon hash browns

3 cups frozen hash brown potatoes, thawed
2 pouches (3 ounces each) smoked salmon*
½ cup chopped onion
½ cup chopped bell pepper
¼ teaspoon black pepper
2 tablespoons vegetable oil

Smoked salmon in foil packages can be found in the canned fish section of the supermarket. Do not substitute lox or other fresh smoked salmon.

1. Combine potatoes, salmon, onion, bell pepper and black pepper in large bowl; mix well.

2. Heat oil in large nonstick skillet over medium-high heat. Add potato mixture; spread to cover surface of skillet. Carefully pat down to avoid oil spatter.

3. Cook 5 minutes or until crisp and browned. Turn over in large pieces. Cook 2 to 3 minutes or until brown. *Makes 4 servings*

classic veg•all® chicken pot pie

2 cans (15 ounces each) VEG•ALL® Original Mixed Vegetables, drained
1 can (10 ounces) cooked chicken, drained
1 can (10¾ ounces) condensed cream of chicken soup, undiluted
¼ teaspoon thyme
¼ teaspoon black pepper
2 (9-inch) frozen ready-to-bake pie crust

1. Preheat oven to 375°F. In medium bowl, combine Veg•All, chicken, soup, and thyme; mix well. Fit one pie crust into 9-inch pie pan; pour vegetable mixture into pie crust. Top with remaining crust; crimp edges to seal and prick top with fork.

2. Bake for 30 to 45 minutes (on lower rack) or until crust is golden brown and filling is hot. Allow pie to cool slightly before cutting into wedges to serve. *Makes 4 servings*

smoked salmon hash browns

octo-dogs and shells

4 hot dogs
1½ cups uncooked small shell pasta
1½ cups frozen mixed vegetables
1 cup prepared Alfredo sauce
Yellow mustard in squeeze bottle
Cheese-flavored fish-shaped crackers

1. Lay 1 hot dog on cutting surface. Starting 1 inch from one end of hot dog, slice hot dog vertically in half. Roll hot dog ¼ turn. Starting 1 inch from same end, slice in half vertically again, making 4 segments connected at top. Slice each segment in half vertically, creating a total of 8 "legs." Repeat with remaining hot dogs.

2. Place hot dogs in medium saucepan; cover with water. Bring to a boil over medium-high heat. Remove from heat; set aside.

3. Prepare pasta according to package directions, stirring in vegetables during last 3 minutes of cooking time. Drain; return to pan. Stir in Alfredo sauce. Heat over low heat until heated through. Divide pasta mixture between 4 plates.

4. Drain octo-dogs. Arrange one octo-dog on top of pasta mixture on each plate. Draw faces on "heads" of octo-dogs with mustard. Sprinkle crackers over pasta. *Makes 4 servings*

octo-dog and shells

ragú® no boiling lasagna

2 containers (15 ounces each) ricotta cheese
2 cups shredded mozzarella cheese (about 8 ounces)
½ cup grated Parmesan cheese
2 eggs
2 jars (1 pound 10 ounces each) RAGÚ® Old World Style® Pasta Sauce
12 uncooked lasagna noodles

1. Preheat oven to 375°F. In bowl, combine ricotta, 1 cup mozzarella, ¼ cup Parmesan cheese and eggs.

2. In 13×9-inch baking dish, spread 1 cup Pasta Sauce. Layer 4 uncooked noodles, then 1 cup sauce and ½ of the ricotta mixture; repeat. Top with remaining 4 uncooked noodles and 2 cups Pasta Sauce. Cover tightly with aluminum foil and bake 1 hour.

3. Remove foil and sprinkle with remaining cheeses. Bake uncovered an additional 10 minutes. Let stand 10 minutes before serving. Serve with remaining Pasta Sauce, heated.   *Makes 12 servings*

Variation: For a twist on a classic, add 1 pound ground beef, cooked, to Pasta Sauce.

Note: Recipe can be halved. Bake in an 11×7-inch baking dish 1 hour. Continue as above, omitting last 10 minutes of baking.

Prep Time: 10 minutes
Cook Time: 70 minutes

ragú® no boiling lasagna

cheese & chile enchiladas

1 package (8 ounces) cream cheese, softened
1 package (8 ounces) shredded Cheddar cheese, divided
1 can (4 ounces) diced mild green chiles, drained
¼ cup sliced green onions
6 (6-inch) flour tortillas
1 cup chunky salsa

1. Preheat oven to 350°F. Lightly spray 11×7-inch baking dish with nonstick cooking spray.

2. Beat cream cheese in medium bowl with electric mixer at medium speed until smooth. Add 1 cup Cheddar cheese, chiles and green onions; beat until blended.

3. Spread ¼ cup cream cheese mixture down center of each tortilla; roll up. Place, seam-side down, in prepared baking dish. Pour salsa over tortillas. Sprinkle with remaining 1 cup Cheddar cheese; cover. Bake 20 to 25 minutes or until heated through. *Makes 6 servings*

chuckwagon bbq rice round-up

1 pound lean ground beef
1 (6.8-ounce) package RICE-A-RONI® Beef Flavor
2 tablespoons margarine or butter
2 cups frozen corn
½ cup prepared barbecue sauce
½ cup (2 ounces) shredded Cheddar cheese

1. In large skillet over medium-high heat, brown ground beef until well cooked. Remove from skillet; drain. Set aside.

2. In same skillet over medium heat, sauté rice-vermicelli mix with margarine until vermicelli is golden brown.

3. Slowly stir in 2½ cups water, corn and Special Seasonings; bring to a boil. Reduce heat to low. Cover; simmer 15 to 20 minutes or until rice is tender.

4. Stir in barbecue sauce and ground beef. Sprinkle with cheese. Cover; let stand 3 to 5 minutes or until cheese is melted. *Makes 4 servings*

calzone italiano

Pizza dough for one 14-inch pizza
1 can (15 ounces) CONTADINA® Pizza Sauce, divided
3 ounces sliced pepperoni *or* ½ **pound crumbled Italian sausage, cooked, drained**
2 tablespoons chopped green bell pepper
1 cup (4 ounces) shredded mozzarella cheese
1 cup (8 ounces) ricotta cheese

1. Divide dough into 4 equal portions. Place on lightly floured, large, rimless cookie sheet. Press or roll out dough to 7-inch circles.

2. Spread 2 tablespoons pizza sauce onto half of each circle to within ½ inch of edge; top with one-fourth each pepperoni, bell pepper and mozzarella cheese.

3. Spoon ¼ cup ricotta cheese onto remaining half of each circle; fold dough over. Press edges together tightly to seal. Cut slits into top of dough to allow steam to escape.

4. Bake in preheated 350°F oven for 20 to 25 minutes or until crusts are golden brown. Meanwhile, heat remaining pizza sauce; serve over calzones.
Makes 4 servings

Note: If desired, 1 large calzone may be made instead of 4 individual calzones. To prepare, shape dough into 1 (13-inch) circle. Spread ½ cup pizza sauce onto half of dough; proceed as above. Bake for 25 minutes.

Prep Time: 15 minutes
Cook Time: 25 minutes

tortilla beef casserole

1 package (about 17 ounces) refrigerated fully cooked beef pot roast in
   gravy*

6 (6-inch) corn tortillas, cut into 1-inch pieces

1 jar (16 ounces) salsa

1½ cups canned or frozen corn kernels

1 cup black or pinto beans, rinsed and drained

1 cup (4 ounces) shredded Mexican cheese blend

*Fully cooked beef pot roast can be found in the refrigerated prepared meats section of the
supermarket.*

1. Preheat oven to 350°F. Lightly spray 11×7-inch casserole or 2-quart
casserole with nonstick cooking spray.

2. Drain and discard gravy from pot roast; cut or shred beef into bite-size
pieces.

3. Combine beef, tortillas, salsa, corn and beans in large bowl; mix well.
Transfer to prepared casserole. Bake 20 minutes or until heated through.
Sprinkle with cheese; bake 5 minutes more or until cheese is melted.

Makes 4 servings

tortilla beef casserole

15-minute chicken and broccoli risotto

1 tablespoon vegetable oil
1 small onion, chopped
2 packages (about 9 ounces each) ready-to-serve yellow rice
2 cups frozen chopped broccoli
1 package (about 6 ounces) refrigerated fully cooked chicken breast strips, cut into pieces
½ cup chicken broth or water

1. Heat oil in large skillet over medium-high heat. Add onion; cook 3 minutes or until translucent.

2. Knead rice in bag. Add rice, broccoli, chicken and broth to skillet. Cover; cook and stir 6 to 8 minutes or until heated through.   *Makes 4 servings*

Serving Suggestion: Top with toasted sliced almonds for a crunchy texture and added flavor.

easy chicken chalupas

1 fully cooked roasted chicken (about 2 pounds)
8 flour tortillas
2 cups shredded Cheddar cheese
1 cup mild green chili salsa
1 cup mild red salsa

1. Preheat oven to 350°F. Spray 13×9-inch ovenproof dish with nonstick cooking spray.

2. Remove skin and bones from chicken; discard. Shred chicken meat.

3. Place 2 tortillas in bottom of prepared dish, overlapping slightly. Layer tortillas with 1 cup chicken, ½ cup cheese and ¼ cup of each salsa. Repeat layers, ending with cheese and salsas.

4. Bake casserole 25 minutes or until bubbly and hot.   *Makes 6 servings*

Tip: Customize this easy main dish with toppings, on the side, such as sour cream, chopped cilantro, sliced black olives, sliced green onions and sliced avocado.

15-minute chicken and broccoli risotto

vegetarian jambalaya

1 tablespoon vegetable oil
½ cup fresh or frozen diced green or red bell pepper
1 can (about 14 ounces) diced tomatoes with chiles
1 package (12 ounces) ground taco/burrito flavor soy meat substitute, crumbled
1 package (about 9 ounces) New Orleans style ready-to-serve jambalaya rice
2 tablespoons water

1. Heat oil in large skillet over medium-high heat. Add bell pepper; cook 3 minutes.

2. Add tomatoes, soy crumbles and rice; mix well. Stir in water. Cook 5 minutes or until heated through.   *Makes 4 servings*

savory italian supper

1 pound ground beef
1 medium green bell pepper, chopped
1 jar (1 pound 10 ounces) RAGÚ® Old World Style® Pasta Sauce
1½ cups water
1¼ cups uncooked regular or parboiled white rice
1 cup shredded mozzarella cheese (about 4 ounces)

1. In 12-inch nonstick skillet, brown ground beef and green pepper over medium-high heat; drain.

2. Stir in Pasta Sauce, water and rice. Bring to a boil over high heat. Reduce heat to low and simmer covered, stirring occasionally, 35 minutes.

3. Sprinkle with cheese and cook, covered, 5 minutes or until cheese is melted.   *Makes 4 servings*

Prep Time: 5 minutes
Cook Time: 40 minutes

vegetarian jambalaya

shrimp and chicken paella

¾ cup ready-to-serve rice

2 cans (about 14 ounces each) diced tomatoes

½ teaspoon ground turmeric *or* 1 teaspoon saffron threads

12 ounces medium raw shrimp, peeled and deveined

2 chicken tenders (about 4 ounces), cut into bite-size chunks

1 cup frozen peas, thawed

1. Preheat oven to 400°F.

2. Lightly coat 8-inch square glass baking dish with nonstick cooking spray. Place rice into baking dish, shaking to distribute evenly.

3. Pour 1 can of tomatoes with juice over rice; sprinkle turmeric over tomatoes. Arrange shrimp and chicken over tomatoes. Top with peas.

4. Drain second can of tomatoes; discard juice. Arrange tomatoes evenly over shrimp and chicken. Cover casserole loosely with foil. Bake 30 minutes. Remove from oven and let stand, covered, 5 minutes. *Makes 6 servings*

Serving Suggestion: Serve with a green salad tossed with mustard vinaigrette and garnished with ½ cup drained, canned corn kernels.

shrimp and chicken paella

fettuccine gorgonzola with sun-dried tomatoes

4 ounces sun-dried tomatoes (not packed in oil)
8 ounces uncooked spinach or tri-color fettuccine
1 cup cottage cheese
½ cup plain yogurt
½ cup (2 ounces) crumbled Gorgonzola cheese
⅛ teaspoon white pepper
   Additional Gorgonzola cheese (optional)

1. Place sun-dried tomatoes in small bowl; cover with hot water. Let stand 15 minutes or until tomatoes are soft. Drain well; cut into strips. Cook pasta according to package directions. Drain well. Cover and keep warm.

2. Meanwhile, process cottage cheese and yogurt in food processor or blender until smooth. Heat cottage cheese mixture in large skillet over low heat. Add Gorgonzola cheese and white pepper; stir until cheese is melted.

3. Add pasta and tomatoes to skillet; toss to coat with sauce. Garnish with additional Gorgonzola cheese; serve immediately.   *Makes 4 servings*

fettuccine gorgonzola with sun-dried tomatoes

meatball bake

1 jar (1 pound 10 ounces) RAGÚ® Chunky Pasta Sauce
2 cups water
2 cups uncooked instant rice
1 cup frozen green peas, thawed
1½ cups shredded mozzarella cheese (about 6 ounces)
1 package (12 ounces) frozen fully cooked cocktail-size meatballs, thawed

1. Preheat oven to 375°F. Spray 13×9-inch glass baking dish with nonstick cooking spray; set aside.

2. In large bowl, combine Pasta Sauce, water, rice, peas, 1 cup cheese and meatballs. Spoon into prepared baking dish.

3. Bake, uncovered, 25 minutes. Sprinkle with remaining ½ cup cheese and bake an additional 5 minutes or until cheese is melted. Let stand 5 minutes before serving.   *Makes 6 servings*

Prep Time: 10 minutes
Cook Time: 30 minutes

beef & blue cheese salad

1 package (10 ounces) mixed green lettuce leaves
4 ounces sliced rare deli roast beef, cut into thin strips
1 large tomato, seeded and coarsely chopped *or* 8 large cherry tomatoes, halved
½ cup (2 ounces) crumbed blue or Gorgonzola cheese
1 cup croutons
½ cup prepared Caesar or Italian salad dressing

1. Combine lettuce, roast beef, tomato, cheese and croutons in large bowl.

2. Drizzle with dressing; toss well. Serve immediately.   *Makes 4 servings*

Serving Suggestion: Serve with warm crusty French bread.

Cook's Notes: Gorgonzola is one of Italy's great cheeses. It has an ivory-colored interior that is streaked with bluish-green veins. Gorgonzola is made from cow's milk and has a creamy savory flavor. It can be found cut into wedges and wrapped in foil in most supermarkets.

country chicken and biscuits

1 can (10¾ ounces) condensed cream of celery soup
⅓ cup milk or water
4 boneless, skinless chicken breast halves, cooked and cut into bite-sized pieces
1 can (14½ ounces) DEL MONTE® Cut Green Beans, drained
1 can (11 ounces) refrigerated biscuits

1. Preheat oven to 375°F.

2. Combine soup and milk in large bowl. Gently stir in chicken and green beans; season with pepper, if desired. Spoon into 11×7-inch or 2-quart microwavable dish.

3. Cover with plastic wrap; slit to vent. Microwave on HIGH 8 to 10 minutes or until heated through, rotating dish once. If using conventional oven, cover with foil and bake at 375°F, 20 to 25 minutes or until hot.

4. Separate biscuit dough into individual biscuits. Immediately arrange biscuits over hot mixture. Bake in conventional oven about 15 minutes or until biscuits are golden brown and baked through.   *Makes 4 servings*

gazebo chicken

4 boneless chicken breast halves (about 1½ pounds)
6 cups torn butter lettuce leaves or mixed baby greens
1 ripe cantaloupe, seeded and cut into 12 wedges
1 large carrot, shredded
½ cup fresh raspberries
⅔ cup prepared honey-mustard salad dressing, divided

1. Preheat broiler. Place chicken, skin side down, on broiler pan rack. Season with salt and pepper. Broil 4 to 5 inches from heat 8 minutes. Turn; sprinkle with salt and pepper. Broil 6 to 8 minutes or until chicken is no longer pink in center. Remove; cool on broiler pan.

2. Place lettuce on large serving platter; arrange cantaloupe and carrot around lettuce.

3. Remove chicken to cutting board. Slice each breast diagonally into thirds; place chicken on lettuce. Scatter raspberries over salad; drizzle with about 2 tablespoons dressing. Serve with remaining dressing.   *Makes 4 servings*

entertaining

green and gold fettuccine with salmon

- 2 cans (6½ ounces each) salmon,* drained
- 2 tablespoons olive oil
- 2 cloves garlic, minced
- ¼ cup minced parsley
- 2 teaspoons minced fresh oregano *or* ½ teaspoon dried oregano leaves
- 2 teaspoons minced fresh basil *or* ½ teaspoon dried basil leaves
- ¼ teaspoon coarsely ground black pepper
- 4 ounces *each* hot, cooked and drained plain and spinach fettuccine
- 2 teaspoons lemon juice
  Blanched matchstick carrots, asparagus spears or broccoli florets (optional)
  Grated Parmesan cheese

Canned tuna can be substituted for the salmon.

Place salmon in medium bowl. With fork, break into large chunks and debone; remove skin, if desired. Heat oil in large skillet over medium-high heat until hot. Cook and stir garlic until golden. Add parsley, oregano, basil and pepper; cook and stir 30 seconds. Pour half of herb sauce over fettuccine; toss gently to coat. Arrange on large, heated platter; keep warm.

Add salmon and lemon juice to remaining sauce. Heat, stirring gently, just until salmon is hot. Spoon over hot fettuccine. Garnish with vegetables, if desired. Serve with Parmesan cheese. *Makes 6 servings*

Favorite recipe from **National Fisheries Institute**

green and gold fettuccine with salmon

pork and corn bread stuffing casserole

½ teaspoon paprika
¼ teaspoon salt
¼ teaspoon garlic powder
¼ teaspoon black pepper
4 bone-in pork chops (about 1¾ pounds)
2 tablespoons butter
1½ cups chopped onion
¾ cup thinly sliced celery
¾ cup matchstick-size carrot strips*
¼ cup chopped fresh parsley
1 can (about 14 ounces) chicken broth
4 cups corn bread stuffing

*You can substitute shredded carrots from the supermarket produce section.

1. Preheat oven to 350°F. Lightly coat 13×9-inch baking dish with nonstick cooking spray; set aside.

2. Combine paprika, salt, garlic powder and pepper in small bowl. Season both sides of pork chops with paprika mixture.

3. Melt butter in large skillet over medium-high heat. Add pork chops. Cook 2 minutes or just until browned; turn over and cook 1 minute longer. Transfer to plate; set aside.

4. Add onion, celery, carrots and parsley to skillet. Cook and stir 4 minutes or until onions are translucent. Add broth; bring to a boil over high heat. Remove from heat; add stuffing and fluff with a fork. Transfer mixture to prepared baking dish. Place browned pork chops on top. Cover; bake 25 minutes or until pork is no longer pink in center.   *Makes 4 servings*

Variation: For a one-skillet meal, use an ovenproof skillet. Place browned pork chops on mixture in skillet, cover and bake as directed.

pork and corn bread stuffing casserole

beef in wine sauce

4 pounds boneless beef chuck roast, cut into 1½- to 2-inch cubes
2 tablespoons garlic powder
2 cans (10¾ ounces each) condensed golden mushroom soup, undiluted
1 can (8 ounces) sliced mushrooms, drained
¾ cup dry sherry
1 envelope (about 1 ounce) dry onion soup mix
1 bag (20 ounces) frozen sliced carrots, thawed

1. Preheat oven to 325°F. Spray heavy 4-quart casserole or Dutch oven with nonstick cooking spray.

2. Sprinkle beef with garlic powder. Place in prepared casserole.

3. Combine canned soup, mushrooms, sherry and dry soup mix in medium bowl. Pour over meat; mix well. Cover; bake 3 hours or until meat is very tender. Add carrots during last 15 minutes of baking.   *Makes 8 servings*

seafood newburg casserole

1 can (10¾ ounces) condensed cream of shrimp soup, undiluted
½ cup half-and-half
1 tablespoon dry sherry
¼ teaspoon ground red pepper
2 cans (6 ounces each) lump crabmeat, drained
3 cups cooked rice
¼ pound medium raw shrimp, peeled and deveined
¼ pound raw bay scallops
1 jar (4 ounces) pimientos, drained and chopped
¼ cup finely chopped parsley

1. Preheat oven to 350°F. Spray 2½-quart casserole with nonstick cooking spray.

2. Whisk together soup, half-and-half, sherry and red pepper in large bowl. Add crabmeat, rice, shrimp, scallops and pimientos; toss well.

3. Transfer mixture to prepared casserole. Cover; bake 25 minutes or until seafood is opaque. Sprinkle with parsley.   *Makes 6 to 8 servings*

beef in wine sauce

spanish braised chicken with green olives and rice

　2 pounds bone-in skinless chicken thighs
　1 teaspoon paprika
　　Nonstick cooking spray
　¾ cup dry sherry
2¼ cups water
　1 can (about 14 ounces) reduced-sodium chicken broth
　¾ cup sliced pimiento-stuffed green olives
1½ teaspoons dried sage
1½ cups uncooked long-grain white rice

1. Sprinkle chicken thighs with paprika. Spray large nonstick skillet with cooking spray; heat over medium-high heat. Cook chicken 3 to 4 minutes on each side or until golden brown.

2. Remove chicken from skillet. Add sherry, stirring to scrape up bits from bottom of skillet. Add water, chicken broth, olives and sage; bring to a boil. Reduce heat to low. Return chicken to skillet. Cover; simmer 10 minutes.

3. Add rice to liquid around chicken; gently stir to distribute evenly in skillet. Cover; simmer 20 to 25 minutes or until liquid is absorbed and rice is tender.

Makes 6 servings

spanish braised chicken with green olives and rice

teriyaki rib dinner

**1 package (about 15 ounces) refrigerated fully cooked pork back ribs
in barbecue sauce**
2 tablespoons vegetable oil
1 large onion, thinly sliced
4 cups frozen Japanese-style stir-fry vegetables
1 can (8 ounces) pineapple chunks, undrained
¼ cup hoisin sauce
2 tablespoons cider vinegar

1. Remove ribs from package; reserve barbecue sauce. Cut into individual ribs; set aside.

2. Heat oil in Dutch oven over medium-high heat. Add onion; cook 3 minutes or until translucent. Add vegetables; cook and stir 4 minutes.

3. Add ribs, reserved sauce, pineapple with juice, hoisin sauce and vinegar to vegetable mixture; mix well. Cover; cook 5 minutes or until heated through. *Makes 4 servings*

*Hoisin sauce is a Chinese condiment that is normally used with
meat and poultry. It's a mixture of soybeans, garlic and chile peppers
that adds a sweet and spicy flavor to Asian cooking.*

teriyaki rib dinner

greek chicken and spinach rice casserole

Nonstick cooking spray
1 cup finely chopped yellow onion
1 package (10 ounces) frozen chopped spinach, thawed and squeezed dry
1 cup uncooked quick-cooking brown rice
1 cup water
¼ teaspoon salt
⅛ teaspoon ground red pepper
¾ pound chicken tenders
2 teaspoons dried Greek seasoning*
½ teaspoon salt-free lemon-pepper seasoning
1 tablespoon olive oil
1 medium lemon, cut into wedges

*Greek seasoning is a combination of oregano, rosemary and sage.

1. Preheat oven to 350°F. Spray 10-inch ovenproof skillet with cooking spray; place over medium heat. Add onion; cook and stir 4 minutes or until translucent. Add spinach, rice, water, salt and red pepper. Stir until well blended.

2. Remove skillet from heat; place chicken tenders on top of mixture in skillet in single layer. Sprinkle with Greek seasoning and lemon-pepper seasoning. Cover with foil. Bake 25 minutes or until chicken is no longer pink in center.

3. Remove foil. Drizzle oil evenly over top. Serve with lemon wedges.

Makes 4 servings

pork with savory apple stuffing

1 package (6 ounces) corn bread stuffing mix
1 can (14½ ounces) chicken broth
1 small apple, peeled, cored and chopped
¼ cup chopped celery
1⅓ cups *French's*® French Fried Onions, divided
4 boneless pork chops, ¾ inch thick (about 1 pound)
½ cup peach-apricot sweet & sour sauce
1 tablespoon *French's*® Honey Dijon Mustard

1. Preheat oven to 375°F. Combine stuffing mix, broth, apple, celery and *⅔ cup* French Fried Onions in large bowl. Spoon into bottom of greased shallow 2-quart baking dish. Arrange chops on top of stuffing.

2. Combine sweet & sour sauce with mustard in small bowl. Pour over pork. Bake 40 minutes or until pork is no longer pink in center.

3. Sprinkle with remaining onions. Bake 5 minutes or until onions are golden. *Makes 4 servings*

Prep Time: 10 minutes
Cook Time: 45 minutes

chile-corn quiche

1 (9-inch) pastry shell, 1½ inches deep

1 can (8¾ ounces) whole kernel corn, drained, *or* 1 cup frozen whole kernel corn, cooked

1 can (4 ounces) diced mild green chiles, drained

¼ cup thinly sliced green onions

1 cup (4 ounces) shredded Monterey Jack cheese

3 eggs

1½ cups half-and-half

½ teaspoon salt

½ teaspoon ground cumin

1. Preheat oven to 450°F. Line pastry shell with foil; partially fill with uncooked beans or rice to weight shell. Bake 10 minutes. Remove foil and beans; continue baking pastry 5 minutes or until lightly browned. Let cool. *Reduce oven temperature to 375°F.*

2. Combine corn, green chiles and green onions in small bowl. Spoon into pastry shell; top with cheese. Whisk eggs, half-and-half, salt and cumin in medium bowl. Pour over cheese. Bake 35 to 45 minutes or until filling is puffed and knife inserted in center comes out clean. Let stand 10 minutes before serving. *Makes 6 servings*

chile-corn quiche

saffron chicken & vegetables

2 tablespoons vegetable oil

6 bone-in skinless chicken thighs

1 bag (16 ounces) frozen mixed vegetables, such as broccoli, red bell peppers, mushrooms and onions, thawed

1 can (about 14 ounces) roasted garlic-flavored chicken broth

1 can (10¾ ounces) condensed cream of chicken soup, undiluted

1 can (10¾ ounces) condensed cream of mushroom soup, undiluted

1 package (about 8 ounces) uncooked saffron yellow rice mix with seasonings

½ cup water

1 teaspoon paprika (optional)

1. Preheat oven to 350°F. Spray 3-quart casserole with nonstick cooking spray; set aside.

2. Heat oil in large skillet over medium heat. Brown chicken on both sides; drain fat.

3. Meanwhile, combine vegetables, chicken broth, soups, rice mix with seasonings and water in large bowl; mix well. Place mixture in prepared casserole. Top with chicken. Sprinkle with paprika, if desired. Cover; bake 1½ hours or until chicken is cooked through (180°F).   *Makes 6 servings*

saffron chicken & vegetables

halibut provençale

Nonstick cooking spray
1 can (about 28 ounces) diced tomatoes
2 cups finely chopped fennel (bulb only)
1 cup finely chopped onion
2 tablespoons minced orange peel
2 teaspoons herbes de Provence*
4 (4-ounce) halibut steaks (½ inch thick)
1 tablespoon olive oil
¼ cup dry bread crumbs
1 tablespoon grated Parmesan cheese
2 cloves garlic, minced
1 teaspoon paprika
½ teaspoon black pepper
¼ teaspoon salt
Minced fresh basil (optional)

Herbes de Provence spice mixes usually contain dried basil, fennel seed, lavender, marjoram, rosemary, sage, summer savory and thyme.

1. Spray 12-inch skillet with cooking spray; heat over medium heat. Add tomatoes, fennel, onion, orange peel and herbes de Provence. Cook and stir 10 minutes.

2. Place halibut over vegetables; sprinkle with oil. Combine bread crumbs, cheese, paprika, garlic, pepper and salt in small bowl. Sprinkle over fish. Cover skillet; cook about 5 to 6 minutes or until fish just begins to flake when tested with fork. Garnish with basil.   *Makes 4 servings*

Tip: To broil, preheat broiler. Place skillet under broiler; broil 1 to 2 minutes or until bread crumb mixture is golden brown. Sprinkle fish with minced basil, if desired.

halibut provençale

southwestern enchiladas

1 can (10 ounces) enchilada sauce, divided
2 packages (about 6 ounces each) refrigerated fully cooked steak strips*
4 (8-inch) flour tortillas
½ cup condensed nacho cheese soup, undiluted *or* ½ cup chile-flavored pasteurized process cheese spread
1½ cups (6 ounces) shredded Mexican cheese blend

Fully cooked steak strips can be found in the refrigerated prepared meats section of the supermarket.

1. Preheat oven to 350°F. Spread half of enchilada sauce in 9-inch square glass baking dish; set aside.

2. Place about 3 ounces steak down center of each tortilla. Top with 2 tablespoons cheese soup. Roll up tortillas; place seam side down in baking dish. Pour remaining enchilada sauce evenly over tortillas. Sprinkle with cheese. Bake 20 to 25 minutes or until heated through. *Makes 4 servings*

new orleans fish soup

1 pound skinless firm fish fillets, such as grouper, cod or haddock
1 can (about 15 ounces) cannellini beans, rinsed and drained
1 can (about 14 ounces) reduced-sodium chicken broth
1 small yellow summer squash, halved lengthwise and sliced (1 cup)
1 tablespoon Cajun seasoning
2 cans (about 14 ounces each) stewed tomatoes, undrained
½ cup sliced green onions
1 teaspoon grated orange peel

1. Cut fish into 1-inch pieces. Refrigerate until needed.

2. Combine beans, broth, squash and Cajun seasoning in large saucepan. Bring to a boil. Reduce heat; cover and simmer 5 minutes.

3. Stir in tomatoes with juice and fish. Bring to a boil. Reduce heat and gently simmer, covered, 3 to 5 minutes or until fish just begins to flake when tested with fork. Stir in green onions and orange peel. Ladle into soup bowls.
Makes 4 servings

southwestern enchiladas

apple curry chicken

  4 boneless skinless chicken breasts
  1 cup apple juice, divided
  ¼ teaspoon salt
   Dash black pepper
1½ cups plain croutons
  1 medium apple, chopped
  1 medium onion, chopped
  ¼ cup raisins
  2 teaspoons brown sugar
  1 teaspoon curry powder
  ¾ teaspoon poultry seasoning
  ⅛ teaspoon garlic powder

1. Preheat oven to 350°F. Lightly grease 2-quart baking dish.

2. Arrange chicken breasts in single layer in prepared dish. Combine ¼ cup apple juice, salt and pepper in small bowl. Brush juice mixture over chicken.

3. Combine croutons, apple, onion, raisins, brown sugar, curry powder, poultry seasoning and garlic powder in large bowl. Toss with remaining ¾ cup apple juice.

4. Sprinkle crouton mixture over chicken. Cover with foil; bake 45 minutes or until chicken is no longer pink in center.   *Makes 4 servings*

apple curry chicken

sausage pizza pie casserole

8 ounces mild Italian sausage, casings removed
1 package (13.8 ounces) refrigerated pizza dough
½ cup tomato sauce
2 tablespoons chopped fresh basil *or* 2 teaspoons dried basil
½ teaspoon dried oregano
¼ teaspoon red pepper flakes
3 ounces whole mushrooms, quartered
½ cup thinly sliced red onion
½ cup thinly sliced green bell pepper
½ cup seeded diced tomato
½ cup sliced pitted small black olives
8 slices smoked provolone cheese
2 tablespoons grated Parmesan and Romano blend cheese

1. Preheat oven to 350°F. Lightly coat 13×9-inch baking dish with nonstick cooking spray; set aside.

2. Brown sausage in large skillet over medium-high heat, stirring frequently to break up meat; drain fat.

3. Line prepared dish with pizza dough. Roll down sides of crust to form a rim. Spoon sauce evenly over dough; sprinkle with basil, oregano and pepper flakes. Layer with sausage, mushrooms, onion, bell pepper, tomato, olives and provolone cheese. Bake 32 to 25 minutes or until bottom and sides of crust are golden brown. Sprinkle with cheese blend; let stand 5 minutes before serving. *Makes 4 to 6 servings*

manicotti

1 container (16 ounces) ricotta cheese
2 cups (8 ounces) shredded mozzarella cheese
½ cup cottage cheese
2 eggs, beaten
2 tablespoons grated Parmesan cheese
½ teaspoon minced garlic
   Salt and black pepper
1 package (about 8 ounces) uncooked manicotti shells
1 pound ground beef
1 jar (26 ounces) pasta sauce
2 cups water

1. Combine ricotta cheese, mozzarella cheese, cottage cheese, eggs, Parmesan cheese and garlic in large bowl; mix well. Season with salt and pepper.

2. Fill manicotti shells with cheese mixture; place in 13×9-inch baking dish. Preheat oven to 375°F.

3. Brown ground beef in large skillet over medium-high heat, stirring to break up meat. Drain fat. Stir in pasta sauce and water (mixture will be thin). Pour sauce over filled manicotti shells.

4. Cover with foil; bake 1 hour or until sauce has thickened and shells are tender. *Makes 6 servings*

chicken florentine in minutes

3 cups water

1 cup milk

2 tablespoons butter

2 packages (about 4 ounces each) fettuccine Alfredo or stroganoff pasta mix

4 cups baby spinach, coarsely chopped

¼ teaspoon black pepper

1 package (about 10 ounces) refrigerated fully cooked chicken breast strips, cut into bite-size pieces

¼ cup diced roasted red peppers

¼ cup sour cream

1. Bring water, milk and butter to a boil in large saucepan over medium-high heat. Stir in pasta mixes, spinach and black pepper. Reduce heat to medium. Cook and stir 8 minutes or until pasta is tender.

2. Stir in chicken and red peppers; cook 2 minutes or until hot. Remove from heat. Stir in sour cream.   *Makes 4 servings*

chicken florentine in minutes

asian basil beef and rice

1 package (about 17 ounces) refrigerated fully cooked beef pot roast in gravy or beef tips in gravy

1 tablespoon vegetable oil

2 cups sliced mushrooms

1 pouch (about 9 ounces) teriyaki-flavored ready-to-serve rice

2 tablespoons water

1 tablespoon hoisin sauce or Asian chili garlic sauce

1 teaspoon soy sauce

1 tablespoon sliced green onion

1 tablespoon minced fresh basil

1. Drain and discard gravy from beef; cut roast into 1-inch pieces. Set aside.

2. Heat oil in large skillet over medium-high heat. Add mushrooms; cook and stir 2 to 3 minutes or until lightly browned.

3. Crumble rice in bag. Add rice, beef, water, hoisin sauce and soy sauce to skillet. Cover and cook over medium heat 3 to 5 minutes or until mixture is heated through. Stir in green onion and basil; serve immediately.

Makes 4 servings

souped-up soup

1 can (10 ounces) condensed tomato soup, plus 1½ cans water

⅓ cup sliced carrot

¼ cup uncooked elbow macaroni

¼ cup chopped celery

¼ cup diced zucchini

½ teaspoon Italian seasoning

½ cup croutons

2 tablespoons grated Parmesan cheese

Stir soup and water in medium saucepan over medium heat. Add carrot, elbow macaroni, celery, zucchini and Italian seasoning. Bring to a boil. Reduce heat; simmer 10 minutes or until macaroni is cooked and vegetables are tender. Serve in bowls; top with croutons and Parmesan cheese.

Makes 4 servings

asian basil beef and rice

tuna quesadilla stack

   4 (10-inch) flour tortillas
 ¼ cup plus 2 tablespoons pinto or black bean dip
   1 can (about 14 ounces) diced tomatoes, drained
   1 can (9 ounces) tuna packed in water, drained and flaked
   2 cups (8 ounces) shredded Cheddar cheese
 ½ cup thinly sliced green onions
1½ teaspoons butter or margarine, melted

1. Preheat oven to 400°F.

2. Place 1 tortilla on 12-inch pizza pan. Spread with 2 tablespoons bean dip, leaving ½-inch border. Top with one third each of tomatoes, tuna, cheese and green onions. Repeat layers twice, beginning with tortilla and ending with onions.

3. Top with remaining tortilla, pressing gently. Brush with melted butter.

4. Bake 15 minutes or until cheese melts and top is lightly browned. Cool slightly. Cut into 8 wedges. *Makes 2 servings*

Tip: For a special touch, serve with assorted toppings, such as guacamole, sour cream and salsa.

Prep and Cook Time: 25 minutes

tuna quesadilla stack

broccoli, turkey and noodle skillet

1 tablespoon butter
1 green bell pepper, chopped
1 cup frozen chopped broccoli, thawed
¼ teaspoon black pepper
1½ cups chicken broth
½ cup milk or half-and-half
2 cups diced cooked turkey breast
1 package (about 4 ounces) chicken and broccoli pasta mix
¼ cup sour cream

1. Melt butter in large nonstick skillet over medium-high heat. Add bell pepper, broccoli and black pepper; cook 5 minutes or until bell pepper is crisp-tender. Add chicken broth and milk. Bring to a boil. Stir in turkey and pasta mix.

2. Reduce heat to low. Cook 8 to 10 minutes or until noodles are tender. Remove from heat. Stir in sour cream. Let stand, uncovered, 5 minutes or until sauce is thickened. *Makes 4 servings*

crunchy veg•all® tuna casserole

2 cups cooked medium egg noodles
1 can (15 ounces) VEG•ALL® Original Mixed Vegetables, drained
1 can (12 ounces) solid white tuna in water, drained
1 can (10.75 ounces) condensed cream of celery soup, undiluted
1¼ cups whole milk
½ cup sour cream
1 tablespoon chopped fresh dill
1 cup crushed sour cream & onion potato chips

Combine all ingredients except potato chips in greased 1½-quart casserole dish.

Microwave, uncovered, on High for 10 to 12 minutes or until very thick. Let cool for 10 minutes.

Top with crushed potato chips and serve. *Makes 4 to 6 servings*

broccoli, turkey and noodle skillet

hearty shepherd's pie

1½ pounds ground beef
2 cups *French's*® French Fried Onions
1 can (10¾ ounces) condensed tomato soup
½ cup water
2 teaspoons Italian seasoning
¼ teaspoon *each* salt and black pepper
1 package (10 ounces) frozen mixed vegetables, thawed
3 cups hot mashed potatoes

1. Preheat oven to 375°F. Cook meat in large ovenproof skillet until browned; drain. Stir in *1 cup* French Fried Onions, soup, water, seasoning, salt and pepper.

2. Spoon vegetables over beef mixture. Top with mashed potatoes.

3. Bake 20 minutes or until hot. Sprinkle with remaining onions. Bake 2 minutes or until golden. *Makes 6 servings*

Prep Time: 10 minutes
Cook Time: 27 minutes

curried shrimp and noodles

3 cups water
2 packages (about 1.6 ounces each) instant curry-flavored rice noodle soup mix
1 package (8 ounces) frozen cooked baby shrimp
1 cup frozen bell pepper strips, cut into 1-inch pieces
¼ cup chopped green onions
¼ teaspoon salt
¼ teaspoon black pepper
1 to 2 tablespoons fresh lime juice

1. Bring water to a boil in large saucepan over high heat. Add soup mixes, shrimp, bell pepper, green onions, salt and black pepper.

2. Cook 3 to 5 minutes, stirring frequently, or until noodles are tender. Stir in lime juice. Serve immediately. *Makes 4 servings*

hearty shepherd's pie

turkey paella

1 tablespoon olive oil
1 small onion, chopped
1 clove garlic, minced
8 ounces raw bulk chorizo*
2 cups chicken broth
¼ teaspoon crushed saffron threads or ground turmeric
2 cups diced cooked turkey (preferably dark meat)
½ pound large raw shrimp, peeled and deveined
1 cup converted rice
1 medium tomato, diced
¼ teaspoon salt
   Black pepper
1 cup thawed frozen peas
¼ cup diced pimiento

Chorizo, a spicy Mexican pork sausage, is flavored with garlic and chiles. It's available in most supermarkets, but if you can't find it, substitute 8 ounces bulk pork sausage plus ¼ teaspoon ground red pepper.

1. Heat oil in 12-inch skillet over medium-high heat. Add onion; cook and stir 3 to 5 minutes or until onion is translucent. Add garlic and chorizo; break up with spoon. Brown chorizo. Drain fat.

2. Add chicken broth and saffron; bring to a simmer. Add turkey, shrimp, rice, tomato, salt and pepper. Bring to a boil; scrape up browned bits. Cover; reduce heat. Simmer 20 minutes or until liquid is absorbed and rice is tender (mixture may be slightly soupy). Stir in peas and pimiento. Simmer 2 to 3 minutes to heat through.   *Makes 4 to 6 servings*

asian noodles with vegetables and chicken

1 tablespoon vegetable oil

2 cups sliced shiitake or button mushrooms

2 cups snow peas, sliced diagonally in half

2 packages (1.6 ounces each) garlic and vegetable instant rice noodle soup mix

2 cups boiling water

2 packages (about 6 ounces each) refrigerated fully cooked chicken breast strips, cut into pieces

¼ teaspoon red pepper flakes

2 tablespoons lime juice

1 tablespoon soy sauce

2 tablespoons chopped fresh cilantro or sliced green onion

1. Heat oil in large skillet over medium-high heat. Add mushrooms and snow peas; cook 2 to 3 minutes or until peas are crisp-tender. Remove from skillet; set aside.

2. Break up noodles from soup mixes into skillet. Add 1 seasoning packet, water, chicken and red pepper flakes; mix well. Cook over medium-high heat 5 to 7 minutes or until liquid thickens. Stir in reserved vegetables, lime juice and soy sauce. Sprinkle with cilantro. Serve immediately.

Makes 4 servings

pork and sweet potato skillet

1 teaspoon fennel or caraway seeds

¾ pound pork tenderloin, cut into 1-inch cubes

1 tablespoon plus 1 teaspoon butter, divided

¼ teaspoon salt

⅛ teaspoon black pepper

2 medium sweet potatoes (about 2 cups), peeled and cut into ½-inch pieces

1 small onion, sliced

¼ pound reduced-fat smoked turkey sausage, halved lengthwise and cut into ½-inch pieces

1 small red apple, cored and cut into ½-inch pieces

½ cup prepared sweet and sour sauce

2 tablespoons chopped fresh parsley (optional)

1. Toast seeds in large nonstick skillet over medium heat 30 seconds or just until fragrant.

2. Add pork and 1 teaspoon butter to skillet; cook and stir 2 to 3 minutes or until pork is no longer pink. Season with salt and pepper. Remove from skillet.

3. Add remaining 1 tablespoon butter, potatoes and onion to skillet. Cover; cook and stir over medium-low heat 8 to 10 minutes or until tender.

4. Add pork, sausage, apple and sweet and sour sauce to skillet; cook and stir until heated through. Garnish with parsley.   *Makes 4 servings*

Prep Time: 20 minutes
Cook Time: 12 to 15 minutes

pork and sweet potato skillet

tofu and snow pea noodle bowl

5 cups water

6 tablespoons chicken-flavored broth powder*

4 ounces uncooked vermicelli, broken in thirds

½ pound firm tofu, rinsed, patted dry and cut in ¼-inch cubes

3 ounces fresh or frozen snow peas, whole or slivered

1 cup matchstick-size carrot strips**

½ teaspoon garlic chili sauce

½ cup chopped green onions

¼ cup chopped fresh cilantro (optional)

2 tablespoons lime juice

2 teaspoons soy sauce

1 tablespoon grated fresh ginger

Chicken-flavored vegetarian broth powder can be found in natural food stores and some supermarkets.

**You may substitute shredded carrots from the supermarket produce section.*

1. Bring water to a boil in a large saucepan over high heat. Stir in broth powder and vermicelli. Return to a boil. Reduce heat to medium-high and simmer 6 minutes. Stir in tofu, snow peas, carrot and chili sauce. Simmer 2 minutes.

2. Remove from heat. Stir in green onions, cilantro, if desired, lime juice, soy sauce and ginger. Serve immediately. *Makes 4 servings*

Tip: Substitute an equal amount of canned vegetable broth for the water and broth powder.

tofu and snow pea noodle bowls

zesty chicken succotash

1 (3- to 4-pound) chicken, cut up and skinned, if desired
1 onion, chopped
1 rib celery, sliced
¼ cup *Frank's® RedHot®* Original Cayenne Pepper Sauce
1 package (10 ounces) frozen lima beans
1 package (10 ounces) frozen whole kernel corn
2 tomatoes, coarsely chopped

1. Heat *1 tablespoon oil* in large skillet until hot. Add chicken; cook 10 minutes or until browned on all sides. Drain off all but 1 tablespoon fat. Add onion and celery; cook and stir 3 minutes or until tender.

2. Stir in *¾ cup water*, **Frank's RedHot** Sauce and remaining ingredients. Heat to boiling. Reduce heat to medium-low. Cook, covered, 20 to 25 minutes or until chicken is no longer pink near bone. Sprinkle with chopped fresh parsley, if desired.   *Makes 6 servings*

Prep Time: 10 minutes
Cook Time: 30 minutes

tuna melts

1 can (12 ounces) chunk white tuna packed in water, drained and flaked
1½ cups packaged coleslaw mix
3 tablespoons sliced green onions
3 tablespoons mayonnaise
1 tablespoon Dijon mustard
1 teaspoon dried dill weed
4 English muffins, split and lightly toasted
⅓ cup shredded Cheddar cheese

1. Preheat broiler. Combine tuna, coleslaw mix and green onions in medium bowl. Combine mayonnaise, mustard and dill weed in small bowl. Stir mayonnaise mixture into tuna mixture. Spread tuna mixture onto muffin halves. Place on broiler pan.

2. Broil 4 inches from heat 3 to 4 minutes or until heated through. Sprinkle with cheese. Broil 1 to 2 minutes more or until cheese is melted.
Makes 4 servings

zesty chicken succotash

southwestern turkey stew

1 tablespoon vegetable oil
1 small onion, finely chopped
1 clove garlic, minced
2 cups reduced-sodium chicken broth
2 cups cooked smoked turkey breast, cut into ½-inch pieces
2 cups frozen corn kernels
1 can (about 14 ounces) diced tomatoes
1 package (about 6 ounces) red beans and rice mix
1 to 2 canned chipotle peppers in adobo sauce,* drained and minced
  Chopped green onion (optional)

Canned chipotle peppers can be found in the Mexican section of most supermarkets or gourmet food stores. Chipotle peppers can sting and irritate the skin, so wear rubber gloves when handling peppers and do not touch your eyes.

1. Heat oil in large nonstick skillet over medium-high heat. Add onion and garlic; cook and stir 3 minutes or until onion is translucent.

2. Add broth; bring to a boil. Stir in turkey, corn, tomatoes, bean mix and chipotle pepper. Reduce heat to low. Cover; cook 10 to 12 minutes or until rice is tender. Let stand 3 minutes. Garnish with green onion.

Makes 4 servings

Substitutions: Use ¼ teaspoon chipotle chili powder and 1 minced jalapeño pepper in place of the chipotle pepper.

southwestern turkey stew

chicken parmesan pasta toss

1 jar (1 pound 10 ounces) RAGÚ® Organic Pasta Sauce
8 ounces fusilli, bucati or your favorite pasta, cooked and drained
1 package (12 ounces) baked breaded low fat chicken breast tenders, heated according to package directions
2 cups shredded mozzarella cheese (about 8 ounces)

1. In 2-quart saucepan, heat Pasta Sauce.

2. In large serving bowl, combine hot Pasta Sauce, pasta, chicken and 1 cup cheese. Top with remaining 1 cup cheese and serve immediately.

Makes 4 servings

Prep Time: 20 minutes

quick chicken jambalaya

8 boneless skinless chicken thighs, cut into bite-size pieces
¼ teaspoon garlic salt
1 tablespoon vegetable oil
2½ cups 8-vegetable juice
1 bag (16 ounces) frozen pepper stir-fry mix
½ cup diced cooked ham
1 teaspoon hot pepper sauce
1¾ cups uncooked quick cooking rice

Sprinkle chicken with garlic salt. In large nonstick skillet, place oil and heat over medium-high heat. Add chicken and cook, stirring occasionally, 8 minutes or until chicken is lightly browned. Add vegetable juice, pepper stir-fry mix, ham and hot pepper sauce. Heat to boiling; cover and cook over medium heat 4 minutes. Stir in rice; heat to boiling. Cover; remove pan from heat and let stand 5 minutes or until rice and vegetables are tender and liquid is absorbed.

Makes 4 servings

Favorite recipe from **Delmarva Poultry Industry, Inc.**

chicken parmesan pasta toss

cuban-style black bean soup

2 teaspoons olive oil
1 small onion, chopped
1 cup thinly sliced carrots
2 jalapeño peppers,* seeded and minced
2 cloves garlic, minced
1 can (about 15 ounces) black beans, undrained
1 can (about 14 ounces) vegetable or chicken broth
¼ cup sour cream
¼ cup chopped fresh cilantro
4 lime wedges (optional)

Jalapeño peppers can sting and irritate the skin, so wear rubber gloves when handling peppers and do not touch your eyes.

1. Heat oil in large saucepan over medium heat. Add onion, carrots, jalapeño pepper and garlic; cook and stir 5 minutes.

2. Add beans and broth; bring to a boil. Cover; reduce heat and simmer 15 to 20 minutes or until vegetables are very tender.

3. Ladle soup into shallow bowls; top with sour cream and cilantro. Serve with lime wedges.   *Makes 4 servings*

Note: Soup will be chunky. If desired, process soup in food processor or blender until smooth.

smoky mountain chicken and rice casserole

Vegetable cooking spray
2 cups sour cream
1 (10¾-ounce) can condensed cream of chicken soup
2 canned chipotle peppers in adobo sauce, finely chopped
1 teaspoon salt
1 teaspoon pepper
3 cups cooked rice
2 cups shredded cooked chicken
2 cups shredded smoked cheddar cheese

Preheat oven to 400°F. Lightly coat 13×9×2-inch baking dish with vegetable cooking spray. In large bowl, stir together sour cream, soup, chipotles, salt and pepper until well blended. Stir in rice, chicken and cheese. Spoon into baking dish. Bake uncovered in preheated oven 20 to 25 minutes, until edges of casserole are bubbly. Turn oven to broil setting and lightly brown casserole. *Makes 8 to 10 servings*

Favorite recipe from **USA Rice**

pizza meatball and noodle soup

1 can (about 14 ounces) reduced-sodium beef broth
½ cup chopped onion
½ cup chopped carrot
2 ounces uncooked whole wheat spaghetti, broken into 3-inch pieces
1 cup zucchini slices, cut in half
8 ounces frozen fully-cooked Italian-style meatballs, thawed
1 can (8 ounces) tomato sauce
½ cup (2 ounces) shredded part-skim mozzarella cheese

1. Combine broth, onion and carrot in large saucepan. Add spaghetti. Bring to a boil. Reduce heat; cover and simmer 3 minutes.

2. Add zucchini, meatballs and tomato sauce to broth mixture. Return to a boil. Reduce heat. Cover and simmer 8 to 9 minutes more or until meatballs are hot and spaghetti is tender, stirring frequently. Ladle into bowls. Sprinkle with mozzarella cheese. *Makes 4 servings*

weeknight suppers

hearty beef and potato casserole

1 package (about 17 ounces) refrigerated fully cooked beef pot roast in gravy*

3 cups frozen hash brown potatoes, divided

¼ teaspoon salt

¼ teaspoon black pepper

1 can (about 14 ounces) diced tomatoes

½ cup canned chipotle chile sauce

1 cup (4 ounces) shredded sharp Cheddar cheese

*Fully cooked beef pot roast can be found in the refrigerated prepared meats section of the supermarket.

1. Preheat oven to 375°F. Grease 11×7-inch glass baking dish.

2. Drain and discard gravy from pot roast. Cut beef into ¼-inch thick slices; set aside. Place 2 cups potatoes in prepared baking dish. Sprinkle with salt and pepper. Top with beef. Combine tomatoes and chile sauce in small bowl; spread evenly over beef. Top with remaining potatoes. Sprinkle with cheese.

3. Lightly cover dish with foil. Bake 20 minutes. Remove foil; bake 20 minutes longer or until hot and bubbly. Let stand 5 to 10 minutes before serving.

Makes 6 servings

hearty beef and potato casserole

empanada pie

1 tablespoon vegetable oil
1 small onion, chopped
1 pound ground beef chuck
1 package (about 1 ounce) taco seasoning mix
1 can (8 ounces) tomato sauce
¼ cup raisins
2 teaspoons dark brown sugar
1 package (8 count) refrigerated crescent rolls
   Sliced green onion (optional)

1. Preheat oven to 375°F. Grease 10-inch shallow round baking dish or deep-dish pie plate.

2. Heat oil in large skillet over medium-high heat. Add onion; cook 2 to 3 minutes or until translucent. Add ground beef; brown 6 to 8 minutes, stirring to break up meat. Drain fat. Sprinkle taco seasoning over beef mixture. Add tomato sauce, raisins and brown sugar. Reduce heat to low; cook 2 to 3 minutes.

3. Spoon beef mixture into prepared dish. Unroll crescent dough; divide into triangles. Arrange with points of dough towards center. Do not seal dough pieces together.

4. Bake 13 to 17 minutes or until dough is puffed and golden brown. Garnish with green onion. *Makes 4 to 6 servings*

empanada pie

southern pork barbecue dinner

  1 tablespoon vegetable oil
½ cup chopped onion
½ cup chopped celery
½ cup chopped green bell pepper
  1 container (about 18 ounces) refrigerated fully-cooked shredded pork
  1 can (about 15 ounces) pinto beans or black-eyed peas, rinsed and
     drained
  1 can (8 ounces) tomato sauce
  2 tablespoons Dijon mustard

1. Heat oil in large skillet over medium-high heat. Add onion, celery and bell pepper; cook and stir 5 minutes or until tender.

2. Stir in pork, beans, tomato sauce and mustard. Cook over low heat 5 to 10 minutes or until heated through. *Makes 4 to 6 servings*

Variation: To make a sandwich, omit the beans and serve on buns.

creamy chicken and veggie soup

  2 cans (10¾ ounces each) condensed cream of chicken soup, undiluted
2¾ cups reduced-sodium chicken broth
  3 medium Yukon gold potatoes, peeled and diced
  1 cup finely chopped green onions, divided
  2 cups cooked diced chicken
  1 package (10 ounces) frozen green peas and carrots
¼ cup half-and-half or whole milk

1. Place soup, broth, potatoes and ½ cup green onions into large saucepan. Increase heat to high; bring just to a boil. Reduce heat; cover and simmer 15 minutes or until potatoes are tender.

2. Remove from heat; stir in chicken, peas and carrots and half-and-half. Cook until peas and carrots are heated through. Sprinkle with remaining ½ cup green onions. *Makes 6 servings*

southern pork barbecue dinner

portuguese potato & greens soup

2 tablespoons olive oil
1 cup chopped onion
1 cup chopped carrots
2 cloves garlic, minced
1 pound new red potatoes, unpeeled, cut into 1-inch pieces
2 cups water
1 can (about 14 ounces) chicken broth
¼ teaspoon salt
½ pound chorizo sausage, casings removed
½ pound kale
  Additional salt (optional)
  Black pepper (optional)

1. Heat oil in large saucepan over medium heat. Add onion, carrots and garlic; cook and stir 5 to 6 minutes or until lightly browned. Add potatoes, water, chicken broth and ¼ teaspoon salt. Bring to a boil. Reduce heat to low. Cover; simmer 10 to 15 minutes or until potatoes are tender. Cool slightly.

2. Meanwhile, heat large nonstick skillet over medium heat. Crumble chorizo into skillet. Cook and stir 5 to 6 minutes or until sausage is cooked through. Drain sausage on paper towels.

3. Wash kale; remove tough stems. Slice into thin shreds.

4. Add sausage and kale to broth mixture; cook, uncovered, 4 to 5 minutes over medium heat until heated through. Kale should be bright green and slightly crunchy. Season with additional salt and pepper, if desired.

Makes 4 servings

portuguese potato & greens soup

classic turkey pot pie

2 cans (15 ounces each) VEG•ALL® Original Mixed Vegetables, drained
1 can (10¾ ounces) condensed cream of potato soup, undiluted
¼ cup milk
1 pound cooked turkey, shredded (2 cups)
¼ teaspoon dried thyme
¼ teaspoon black pepper
2 (9-inch) refrigerated ready-to-bake pie crusts

Preheat oven to 375°F. In medium mixing bowl, combine first 6 ingredients; mix well. Place 1 pie crust into 9-inch pie pan; pour vegetable mixture into pie crust. Top with remaining crust, crimp edges to seal, and slit top with knife. Bake for 50 to 60 minutes (on lower rack) or until crust is golden brown and filling is hot. Allow pie to cool slightly before cutting into wedges to serve. *Makes 8 servings*

lemon shrimp

1 package (12 ounces) uncooked egg noodles
½ cup (1 stick) butter, softened
2 pounds medium cooked shrimp
3 tomatoes, chopped
1 cup shredded carrots
1 cup chicken broth
1 can (4 ounces) sliced mushrooms, drained
2 tablespoons lemon juice
2 cloves garlic, chopped
½ teaspoon celery seed
¼ teaspoon black pepper

1. Preheat oven to 350°F.

2. Cook noodles according to package directions. Drain; toss with butter in large bowl until butter is melted and noodles are evenly coated. Stir in remaining ingredients. Transfer to 3-quart casserole.

3. Bake 15 to 20 minutes or until heated through. *Makes 8 servings*

classic turkey pot pie

delicious ham & cheese puff pie

2 cups (about 1 pound) diced cooked ham
1 package (10 ounces) frozen chopped spinach, thawed and squeezed dry
½ cup diced red bell pepper
4 green onions, sliced
3 eggs
¾ cup all-purpose flour
¾ cup (3 ounces) shredded Swiss cheese
¾ cup milk
1 tablespoon prepared mustard
1 teaspoon grated lemon peel
1 teaspoon dried dill weed
½ teaspoon garlic salt
½ teaspoon black pepper
  Fresh dill sprigs and lemon slices (optional)

1. Preheat oven to 425°F. Grease round 2-quart casserole.

2. Combine ham, spinach, bell pepper and green onions in prepared casserole.

3. Beat eggs in medium bowl. Add flour, cheese, milk, mustard, lemon peel, dill weed, garlic salt and black pepper; stir until combined. Pour egg mixture over ham mixture.

4. Bake 30 to 35 minutes or until puffed and browned. Cut into wedges and garnish with fresh dill and lemon slices.   *Makes 4 to 6 servings*

delicious ham & cheese puff pie

hearty pork, apple and noodle skillet

2 apples, such as Fuji, Gala or Golden Delicious, peeled and cored
2 tablespoons butter, divided
1 small onion, finely chopped
1 package (about 27 ounces) garlic and herb marinated pork loin fillet
1½ cups chicken broth
½ cup milk
1 package (about 4 ounces) stroganoff pasta mix
¼ teaspoon black pepper
¼ cup sour cream

1. Slice apples into ¼-inch-thick slices. Melt 1 tablespoon butter in large nonstick skillet over medium heat. Add apples and onion. Cook 5 to 10 minutes or until apples are lightly browned. Remove to small bowl; set aside.

2. Cut half of pork loin into ½-inch-thick slices. (Reserve remaining pork for another meal.) Melt remaining 1 tablespoon butter in skillet over medium heat. Brown pork in 2 batches, 2 to 3 minutes per side. Do not overcook. Remove to warm platter; repeat with remaining pork.

3. Place broth and milk in skillet; bring to a boil. Add pasta mix, apple mixture and pepper; mix well. Cook over medium heat 10 minutes or until noodles are tender and sauce is slightly thickened. Stir in sour cream. Serve with pork. *Make 4 servings*

hearty pork, apple and noodle skillet

cajun chicken and rice

4 chicken drumsticks, skin removed
4 chicken thighs, skin removed
2 teaspoons Cajun seasoning
¾ teaspoon salt, divided
2 tablespoons vegetable oil
1 can (about 14 ounces) chicken broth
1 cup uncooked rice
1 medium green bell pepper, coarsely chopped
1 medium red bell pepper, coarsely chopped
½ cup finely chopped green onions
2 cloves garlic, minced
½ teaspoon dried thyme
¼ teaspoon ground turmeric

1. Preheat oven to 350°F. Lightly coat 13×9-inch baking dish with nonstick cooking spray; set aside.

2. Rinse and pat dry chicken pieces. Sprinkle both sides with Cajun seasoning and ¼ teaspoon salt. Heat oil in large skillet over medium-high heat. Add chicken; cook 8 to 10 minutes or until browned on all sides. Transfer to plate; set aside.

3. Add broth to skillet. Bring to a boil, scraping bottom and sides of pan. Add remaining ingredients. Stir well. Pour into prepared baking dish. Place browned chicken on top. Cover tightly with foil. Bake 1 hour or until chicken is cooked through (180°F). *Makes 6 servings*

Variation: For a one-skillet meal, use an ovenproof skillet. Place browned chicken on mixture in skillet, cover, and bake as directed.

cajun chicken and rice

vegetable casserole

1 package (about 16 ounces) frozen spinach
¾ cup (1½ sticks) butter, divided
    Salt and black pepper
8 potatoes, peeled and cooked until tender
1 cup milk
1 pound carrots, sliced and cooked until tender
1 pound green beans, cut into 1-inch pieces and cooked until tender
½ teaspoon paprika

1. Preheat oven to 375°F. Lightly grease 4-quart casserole or roasting pan.

2. Cook spinach according to package directions; drain. Spread spinach in prepared casserole; dot with 1 tablespoon butter and season with salt and pepper.

3. Mash potatoes with milk and ½ cup butter until creamy.

4. Layer half of potatoes, carrots and beans over spinach. Dot with another 1 tablespoon butter; season with salt and pepper.

5. Top with remaining potatoes. Dot with remaining 2 tablespoons butter and sprinkle with paprika. Bake 1 hour or until heated through and lightly browned. *Makes 10 to 12 servings*

vegetable casserole

chipotle turkey strata

6 to 8 (½-inch-thick) Italian bread slices

2 tablespoons chipotle sauce*

2 cups chopped cooked dark turkey meat

1½ cups shredded Cheddar or pepper jack cheese, divided

5 eggs

2½ cups milk

½ teaspoon salt

¼ teaspoon pepper

If you can't find chipotle sauce, substitute 1 tablespoon tomato sauce mixed with 1 tablespoon adobo sauce with chipotles.

1. Preheat oven to 325°F. Grease 9-inch square baking pan. Arrange 3 to 4 bread slices to cover bottom of pan. Cut bread to fit, if necessary. Spread chipotle sauce over bread. Spread turkey over sauce. Sprinkle 1 cup cheese over turkey. Cover with remaining 3 to 4 bread slices.

2. Beat together eggs, milk, salt and pepper. Pour over bread; press down firmly so bread absorbs liquid. Top with remaining ½ cup cheese. Bake 60 to 70 minutes or until set and golden brown. Remove from oven. Let stand 10 to 15 minutes before cutting.   *Makes 6 servings*

Tip: This dish can be assembled up to 8 hours in advance. Cover with foil and chill. Bake a few minutes longer, if necessary.

chipotle turkey strata

veggie beef skillet soup

12 ounces 95% lean ground beef
1 tablespoon olive oil
2 cups coarsely chopped cabbage
1 cup chopped green bell pepper
2 cups water
1 can (about 14 ounces) stewed tomatoes
1 cup frozen mixed vegetables
⅓ cup ketchup
1 tablespoon beef bouillon granules
2 teaspoons Worcestershire sauce
2 teaspoons balsamic vinegar
⅛ teaspoon red pepper flakes
¼ cup chopped fresh parsley

1. Brown beef in large skillet over medium-high heat, stirring to break up meat. Set aside on plate. Add oil, cabbage and bell pepper to skillet; cook and stir 4 minutes or until cabbage is wilted.

2. Add beef, water, tomatoes, vegetables, ketchup, bouillon granules, Worcestershire, vinegar and red pepper flakes; bring to a boil. Reduce heat; cover and simmer 20 minutes. Remove from heat; cover and let stand 5 minutes. Stir in parsley before serving. *Makes 4 servings*

veggie beef skillet soup

spinach & turkey skillet

½ **pound turkey breast tenderloin**
⅛ **teaspoon salt**
2 **teaspoons olive oil**
¼ **cup chopped onion**
2 **cloves garlic, minced**
⅓ **cup uncooked rice**
¾ **teaspoon Italian seasoning**
¼ **teaspoon black pepper**
1 **cup reduced-sodium chicken broth, divided**
2 **cups packed torn stemmed spinach**
⅔ **cup diced plum tomatoes**
3 **tablespoons freshly grated Parmesan cheese**

1. Cut turkey tenderloin into bite-size pieces; sprinkle with salt.

2. Heat oil in medium skillet over medium-high heat. Add turkey pieces; cook and stir until lightly browned. Remove from skillet. Reduce heat to low. Add onion and garlic; cook and stir until tender. Return turkey to skillet. Stir in rice, Italian seasoning and pepper.

3. Reserve 2 tablespoons chicken broth. Stir remaining broth into mixture in skillet. Bring to a boil. Reduce heat; cover and simmer 14 minutes. Stir in spinach and reserved broth. Cover; cook 2 to 3 minutes or until liquid is absorbed and spinach is wilted. Stir in tomatoes; heat through. Serve with Parmesan cheese. *Makes 2 servings*

corned beef hash

2 large russet potatoes, peeled and cut into ½-inch cubes
½ teaspoon salt
¼ teaspoon black pepper
¼ cup (½ stick) butter or margarine
1 large onion, chopped
½ pound corned beef, finely chopped
1 tablespoon prepared horseradish
¼ cup whipping cream (optional)
4 poached or fried eggs

1. Place potatoes in 10-inch skillet. Cover potatoes with water. Bring to a boil over high heat. Reduce heat to low; simmer 6 minutes. (Potatoes will be firm.) Drain potatoes in colander; sprinkle with salt and pepper.

2. Wipe out skillet with paper towel. Add butter and onion; cook and stir over medium-high heat 5 minutes. Stir in corned beef, horseradish and potatoes; mix well. Press down mixture with spatula to flatten into compact layer.

3. Reduce heat to low. Drizzle cream evenly over mixture, if desired. Cook 10 to 15 minutes. Turn mixture with spatula; pat down and continue cooking 10 to 15 minutes or until bottom is well browned. Top each serving with 1 poached egg. Serve immediately. *Makes 4 servings*

slow cooker favorites

sweet potato stew

1 cup chopped onion
1 cup chopped celery
1 cup grated peeled sweet potato
1 cup vegetable broth or water
2 slices bacon, crisp-cooked and crumbled
1 cup half-and-half
  Black pepper
¼ cup minced fresh parsley

Slow Cooker Directions

1. Place onion, celery, sweet potato, broth and bacon in 3-quart slow cooker. Cover; cook on LOW 6 hours or until vegetables are tender.

2. Increase heat to HIGH. Add half-and-half. Add water, if necessary, to reach desired consistency. Cook 30 minutes on HIGH or until heated through.

3. Season with pepper. Stir in parsley.

Makes 4 servings

sweet potato stew

southwestern stuffed peppers

4 green bell peppers
1 can (about 15 ounces) black beans, rinsed and drained
1 cup (4 ounces) shredded pepper-jack cheese
¾ cup medium salsa
½ cup frozen corn
½ cup chopped green onions
⅓ cup uncooked long-grain converted white rice
1 teaspoon chili powder
½ teaspoon ground cumin
   Sour cream

Slow Cooker Directions

1. Cut thin slice off top of each bell pepper. Carefully remove seeds, leaving pepper whole.

2. Combine beans, cheese, salsa, corn, green onions, rice, chili powder and cumin in medium bowl. Spoon filling evenly into each pepper. Place peppers in slow cooker. Cover; cook on LOW 4 to 6 hours. Serve with sour cream.

Makes 4 servings

Prep Time: 15 minutes
Cook Time: 4 to 6 hours

southwestern stuffed peppers

mushroom barley stew

1 tablespoon olive oil
1 medium onion, finely chopped
1 cup chopped carrots (about 2 carrots)
1 clove garlic, minced
5 cups vegetable broth
1 cup uncooked pearl barley
1 cup dried wild mushrooms, broken into pieces
1 teaspoon salt
½ teaspoon dried thyme
½ teaspoon black pepper

Slow Cooker Directions

1. Heat oil in medium skillet over medium-high heat. Add onion, carrots and garlic; cook and stir 5 minutes or until tender. Place in slow cooker.

2. Add broth, barley, mushrooms, salt, thyme and pepper to slow cooker.

3. Cover; cook on LOW 6 to 7 hours. Adjust seasonings.

Makes 4 to 6 servings

Variation: To turn this hearty stew into a soup, add an additional 2 to 3 cups of broth. Cook the same length of time.

Prep Time: 10 minutes
Cook Time: 6 to 7 hours

mushroom barley stew

three-bean mole chili

1 can (about 15 ounces) chili beans in spicy sauce
1 can (about 15 ounces) pinto beans, rinsed and drained
1 can (about 15 ounces) black beans, rinsed and drained
1 can (about 14 ounces) Mexican or chili-style diced tomatoes
1 large green bell pepper, diced
1 small onion, diced
½ cup beef, chicken or vegetable broth
¼ cup prepared mole paste*
2 teaspoons ground cumin
2 teaspoons chili powder
2 teaspoons ground coriander (optional)
2 teaspoons minced garlic
   Toppings: crushed tortilla chips, chopped cilantro or shredded cheese

Mole paste is available in the Mexican section of large supermarkets or in specialty markets.

Slow Cooker Directions

1. Combine beans, tomatoes, bell pepper, onion, broth, mole paste, cumin, chili powder, coriander, if desired, and garlic in slow cooker; mix well.

2. Cover; cook on LOW 5 to 6 hours.

3. Serve with desired toppings.   *Makes 4 to 6 servings*

Prep Time: 10 minutes
Cook Time: 5 to 6 hours

three-bean mole chili

chicken stew

4 to 5 cups chopped cooked chicken (about 5 boneless skinless chicken breasts)
1 can (about 28 ounces) whole tomatoes, cut up, undrained
2 large potatoes, cut into 1-inch pieces
8 ounces fresh okra, sliced
1 large onion, chopped
1 can (14 ounces) cream-style corn
½ cup ketchup
½ cup barbecue sauce

Slow Cooker Directions

1. Combine chicken, tomatoes with juice, potatoes, okra and onion in slow cooker. Cover; cook on LOW 6 to 8 hours or until potatoes are tender.

2. Add corn, ketchup and barbecue sauce. Cover; cook on HIGH 30 minutes.

Makes 6 servings

slow cooker pizza casserole

4 jars (14 ounces each) pizza sauce
1½ pounds ground beef
1 pound bulk pork sausage
2 cups (8 ounces) shredded mozzarella cheese
2 cups grated Parmesan cheese
2 cans (4 ounces each) mushroom stems and pieces, drained
2 packages (3 ounces each) sliced pepperoni
½ cup finely chopped onion
½ cup finely chopped green bell pepper
1 clove garlic, minced
1 pound corkscrew pasta, cooked and drained

Slow Cooker Directions

1. Brown beef and sausage in large nonstick skillet over medium-high heat, stirring to break up meat. Drain fat. Place meat in slow cooker. Add all remaining ingredients except pasta; mix well.

2. Cover; cook on LOW 3½ hours or on HIGH 2 hours. Stir in pasta. Cover; cook 15 to 20 minutes or until pasta is heated through.   *Makes 6 servings*

chicken stew

layered mexican-style casserole

2 cans (about 15 ounces each) hominy,* drained
1 can (about 15 ounces) black beans, rinsed and drained
1 can (about 14 ounces) diced tomatoes with garlic, basil and oregano
1 cup thick and chunky salsa
1 can (6 ounces) tomato paste
½ teaspoon ground cumin
3 (9-inch) flour tortillas
2 cups (8 ounces) shredded Monterey Jack cheese
¼ cup sliced black olives

*Hominy is corn that has been treated to remove the germ and hull. It can be found with the canned vegetables or beans in most supermarkets.

Slow Cooker Directions

1. Prepare foil handles (see below). Spray slow cooker with nonstick cooking spray.

2. Combine hominy, beans, tomatoes, salsa, tomato paste and cumin in large bowl.

3. Press one tortilla in bottom of slow cooker. (Edges of tortilla may turn up slightly.) Top with one third of hominy mixture and one third of cheese. Repeat layers. Press remaining tortilla on top. Top with remaining hominy mixture. Set aside remaining cheese.

4. Cover; cook on LOW 6 to 8 hours. Sprinkle with remaining cheese and olives. Cover; let stand 5 minutes. Pull out tortilla stack with foil handles.

Makes 6 servings

Foil Handles: Tear off three 18×2-inch strips of heavy-duty foil or use regular foil folded to double thickness. Crisscross foil strips in spoke design and place into slow cooker to make lifting of tortilla stack easier.

Prep Time: 15 minutes
Cook Time: 6 to 8 hours

beef with apples & sweet potatoes

1 boneless beef chuck shoulder roast (2 pounds)
1 can (40 ounces) sweet potatoes, drained
2 small onions, sliced
2 apples, cored and sliced
½ cup beef broth
2 cloves garlic, minced
1 teaspoon salt
1 teaspoon dried thyme, divided
¾ teaspoon black pepper, divided
1 tablespoon cornstarch
¼ teaspoon ground cinnamon
2 tablespoons cold water

Slow Cooker Directions

1. Trim and discard fat from beef. Cut beef into 2-inch pieces. Place beef, sweet potatoes, onions, apples, beef broth, garlic, salt, ½ teaspoon thyme and ½ teaspoon pepper in 4-quart slow cooker. Cover; cook on LOW 8 to 9 hours.

2. Transfer beef, sweet potatoes and apples to platter; keep warm. Let liquid stand 5 minutes to allow fat to rise. Skim off and discard fat.

3. Stir together cornstarch, remaining ½ teaspoon thyme, ¼ teaspoon pepper, cinnamon and water until smooth; stir into cooking liquid. Cook 15 minutes on HIGH or until juices are thickened. Serve sauce with beef, sweet potatoes and apples. *Makes 6 servings*

Prep Time: 20 minutes
Cook Time: 8 to 9 hours

barley beef stroganoff

2½ **cups vegetable broth or water**
⅔ **cup uncooked pearl barley (not quick-cooking)**
1 **package (8 ounces) sliced fresh mushrooms**
½ **teaspoon dried marjoram**
½ **teaspoon black pepper**
½ **pound ground beef**
½ **cup chopped celery**
½ **cup minced green onions**
¼ **cup half-and-half**
   Minced fresh parsley (optional)

Slow Cooker Directions

1. Place broth, barley, mushrooms, marjoram and pepper in slow cooker. Cover; cook on LOW 6 to 7 hours.

2. Brown beef in large nonstick skillet over medium-high heat 6 to 8 minutes, stirring to break up meat; drain fat. Add celery and green onions; cook and stir 3 minutes. Stir beef mixture and half-and-half into slow cooker mixture. Cover; cook on HIGH 10 to 15 minutes or until beef is hot and vegetables are tender. Garnish with parsley. *Makes 4 servings*

Serving Suggestion: Serve this delicious beef entrée with a vegetable side or salad.

barley beef stroganoff

south-of-the-border macaroni & cheese

5 cups cooked rotini pasta

2 cups (8 ounces) cubed American cheese

1 can (12 ounces) evaporated milk

1 cup (4 ounces) cubed sharp Cheddar cheese

1 can (4 ounces) diced green chiles, drained

2 teaspoons chili powder

2 medium tomatoes, seeded and chopped

5 green onions, sliced

Slow Cooker Directions

1. Combine all ingredients, except tomatoes and green onions in slow cooker; mix well. Cover; cook on HIGH 2 hours, stirring twice.

2. Stir in tomatoes and green onions; continue cooking until heated through.
Makes 4 servings

chicken and stuffing

½ cup all-purpose flour

¾ teaspoon seasoned salt

¾ teaspoon black pepper

4 to 6 boneless skinless chicken breasts (about 1 to 1½ pounds)

¼ cup (½ stick) butter

2 cans (10¾ ounces each) condensed cream of mushroom soup, undiluted

1 package (12 ounces) seasoned stuffing mix, plus ingredients to prepare mix

Slow Cooker Directions

1. Combine flour, seasoned salt and pepper in large resealable food storage bag. Add chicken; seal bag. Shake to coat with flour mixture.

2. Melt butter in large skillet over medium-low heat. Brown chicken on both sides. Place in slow cooker; pour soup over chicken.

3. Prepare stuffing according to package directions, decreasing liquid by half. Arrange stuffing over chicken. Cover; cook on HIGH 3 to 4 hours.
Makes 4 to 6 servings

south-of-the-border macaroni & cheese

caribbean sweet potato & bean stew

2 medium sweet potatoes (about 1 pound), peeled and cut into
    1-inch cubes
2 cups frozen cut green beans
1 can (about 15 ounces) black beans, rinsed and drained
1 can (about 14 ounces) vegetable broth
1 small onion, sliced
2 teaspoons Caribbean jerk seasoning
½ teaspoon dried thyme
¼ teaspoon salt
¼ teaspoon ground cinnamon
⅓ cup slivered almonds, toasted*
    Hot pepper sauce (optional)

*To toast almonds, spread in single layer on baking sheet. Bake in preheated 350°F oven 8 to
10 minutes or until golden brown, stirring frequently.*

Slow Cooker Directions

1. Combine sweet potatoes, green beans, black beans, broth, onion, jerk
seasoning, thyme, salt and cinnamon in slow cooker. Cover; cook on LOW
5 to 6 hours or until vegetables are tender.

2. Serve with almonds and hot pepper sauce, if desired.

Makes 4 servings

Prep Time: 10 minutes
Cook Time: 5 to 6 hours

caribbean sweet potato & bean stew

chicken with italian sausage

10 ounces bulk mild or hot Italian sausage
6 boneless skinless chicken thighs
1 can (about 15 ounces) white beans, rinsed and drained
1 can (about 15 ounces) red beans, rinsed and drained
1 cup chicken broth
1 medium onion, chopped
½ teaspoon salt
¼ teaspoon black pepper
   Chopped fresh parsley (optional)

Slow Cooker Directions

1. Brown sausage in large skillet over medium-high heat, stirring to break up meat. Drain fat. Spoon sausage into slow cooker.

2. Trim fat from chicken. Place chicken, beans, broth, onion, salt and pepper in slow cooker. Cover; cook on LOW 5 to 6 hours.

3. Slice each chicken thigh on the diagonal. Serve with sausage and beans. Garnish with parsley. *Makes 6 servings*

Prep Time: 15 minutes
Cook Time: 5 to 6 hours

glazed pork loin

1 bag (1 pound) baby carrots
4 boneless pork loin chops
1 jar (8 ounces) apricot preserves

Slow Cooker Directions

1. Place carrots on bottom of slow cooker. Place pork on carrots; spread with preserves.

2. Cover; cook on LOW 8 hours or on HIGH 4 hours. *Makes 4 servings*

Serving Suggestion: Serve with seasoned or cheese-flavored instant mashed potatoes.

chicken with italian sausage

hearty lentil and root vegetable stew

2 cans (about 14 ounces each) chicken broth
1½ cups cubed turnip (1 inch)
1 cup dried red lentils, rinsed and sorted
1 medium onion, cut into ½-inch wedges
2 medium carrots, cut into 1-inch pieces
1 medium red bell pepper, cut into 1-inch pieces
½ teaspoon dried oregano
⅛ teaspoon red pepper flakes
1 tablespoon olive oil
½ teaspoon salt
4 slices bacon, crisp-cooked and crumbled
½ cup finely chopped green onions

Slow Cooker Directions

1. Combine broth, turnip, lentils, onion, carrots, bell pepper, oregano and pepper flakes in 3½- to 4-quart slow cooker. Cover; cook on LOW 6 hours or on HIGH 3 hours or until lentils are cooked.

2. When lentils are tender, stir in olive oil and salt. Sprinkle each serving with bacon and green onions. *Makes 8 servings*

Prep time: 15 minutes

hearty lentil and root vegetable stew

slow cooker salmon with beer

4 salmon fillets (6 ounces each)
  Salt and black pepper
1 cup Italian dressing
3 tablespoons olive oil
1 red bell pepper, sliced
1 yellow bell pepper, sliced
1 orange bell pepper, sliced
1 large onion, sliced
½ teaspoon dried basil
2 cloves garlic, minced
1 teaspoon lemon peel
2 cups spinach, washed and stems removed
¾ cup amber beer
½ lemon, cut into 4 wedges
  Additional salt and black pepper (optional)

Slow Cooker Directions

1. Rinse salmon fillets and pat dry with paper towels. Season both sides of fillets with salt and pepper. Place in casserole dish and pour Italian dressing over fillets. Cover with plastic wrap and refrigerate 30 minutes, or up to 2 hours. Discard marinade.

2. Pour olive oil into 5-quart slow cooker and lay salmon fillets on top, stacking as necessary. Cover with peppers, onion, basil, garlic and lemon peel. Cover with spinach. Pour beer over top. Cover; cook on HIGH 1½ hours.

3. Remove fillets to platter and top with vegetables. Squeeze lemon over salmon and season with additional salt and pepper, if desired.

Makes 4 servings

acknowledgments

The publisher would like to thank the companies listed below for the use of their recipes in this publication.

Delmarva Poultry Industry, Inc.

Del Monte Corporation

The Golden Grain Company®

National Fisheries Institute

Reckitt Benckiser Inc.

Unilever

USA Rice Federation™

Veg•All®

metric conversion chart

VOLUME MEASUREMENTS (dry)

$1/8$ teaspoon = 0.5 mL
$1/4$ teaspoon = 1 mL
$1/2$ teaspoon = 2 mL
$3/4$ teaspoon = 4 mL
1 teaspoon = 5 mL
1 tablespoon = 15 mL
2 tablespoons = 30 mL
$1/4$ cup = 60 mL
$1/3$ cup = 75 mL
$1/2$ cup = 125 mL
$2/3$ cup = 150 mL
$3/4$ cup = 175 mL
1 cup = 250 mL
2 cups = 1 pint = 500 mL
3 cups = 750 mL
4 cups = 1 quart = 1 L

VOLUME MEASUREMENTS (fluid)

1 fluid ounce (2 tablespoons) = 30 mL
4 fluid ounces ($1/2$ cup) = 125 mL
8 fluid ounces (1 cup) = 250 mL
12 fluid ounces ($1 1/2$ cups) = 375 mL
16 fluid ounces (2 cups) = 500 mL

WEIGHTS (mass)

$1/2$ ounce = 15 g
1 ounce = 30 g
3 ounces = 90 g
4 ounces = 120 g
8 ounces = 225 g
10 ounces = 285 g
12 ounces = 360 g
16 ounces = 1 pound = 450 g

DIMENSIONS

$1/16$ inch = 2 mm
$1/8$ inch = 3 mm
$1/4$ inch = 6 mm
$1/2$ inch = 1.5 cm
$3/4$ inch = 2 cm
1 inch = 2.5 cm

OVEN TEMPERATURES

250°F = 120°C
275°F = 140°C
300°F = 150°C
325°F = 160°C
350°F = 180°C
375°F = 190°C
400°F = 200°C
425°F = 220°C
450°F = 230°C

BAKING PAN SIZES

Utensil	Size in Inches/Quarts	Metric Volume	Size in Centimeters
Baking or Cake Pan (square or rectangular)	8×8×2	2 L	20×20×5
	9×9×2	2.5 L	23×23×5
	12×8×2	3 L	30×20×5
	13×9×2	3.5 L	33×23×5
Loaf Pan	8×4×3	1.5 L	20×10×7
	9×5×3	2 L	23×13×7
Round Layer Cake Pan	8×1½	1.2 L	20×4
	9×1½	1.5 L	23×4
Pie Plate	8×1¼	750 mL	20×3
	9×1¼	1 L	23×3
Baking Dish or Casserole	1 quart	1 L	—
	1½ quart	1.5 L	—
	2 quart	2 L	—